For Tommy

First published in New Zealand by Samantha Armstrong
www.samantharmstrong.com

MY VERY HUNGRY HAPPY TUMMY

Written by Samantha Armstrong
Illustration by Abigail Tan

The warm sun came up,
giving me vitamin D.
I laughed, and I played,
and now I am very hungry.

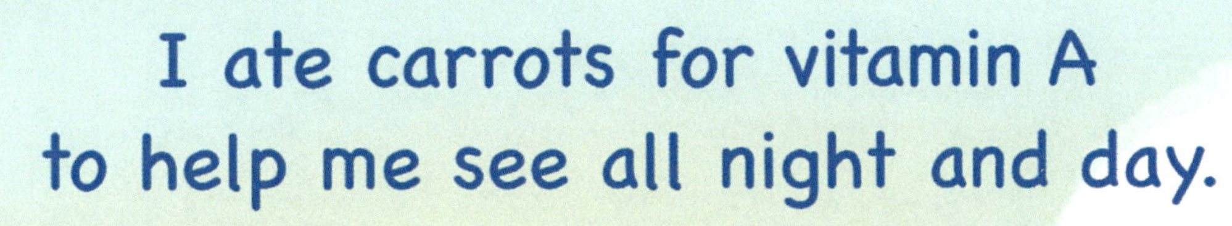

I ate carrots for vitamin A
to help me see all night and day.

I ate oranges for vitamin C
to boost my immunity.

Good immunity helps to keep
tummy aches and colds away.
When you feel unwell and can no longer play,
you can count on your immunity
to save the day!

I ate kale and silverbeet, so green and leafy, to help keep my bones strong and healthy.

I ate bananas and
blueberries,
strawberries
and pears.

I ate tomatoes, cucumbers, and peaches with tiny hairs!

I ate all the fruits and vegetables to look after my body.

Now I am full,
and my tummy is
happy and healthy.

Fun Facts!

Carrots are usually orange, although you can get purple, red, white, and yellow carrots.

Oranges are a citrus fruit, which are picked and eaten in the winter.

Strawberries have lots of vitamin C, and do you remember what that is good for?
. . . Your immunity!

Unlike most fruit, pears ripen best off the tree.

Bananas can float in water.

A single blueberry bush can produce as many as 6000 blueberries per year.

Cucumbers get rid of bad breath.

Some varieties of kale grow
5 to 7 feet tall.

Silverbeet comes in a range of colors,
including pink, red, yellow, green, and white.

There are more than 7500 kinds of
tomatoes grown around the world.

Author's note:

I hope you had a lot of fun
reading about fruits and vegetables.
I can't wait to hear what your favorites are!
Be sure to check out the other books in this series
to learn more about fitness, sleeping,
and how powerful your smile can be!

Made in the USA
Las Vegas, NV
03 June 2024